DATE			

EUTHANASIA

The Debate Over the Right to Die

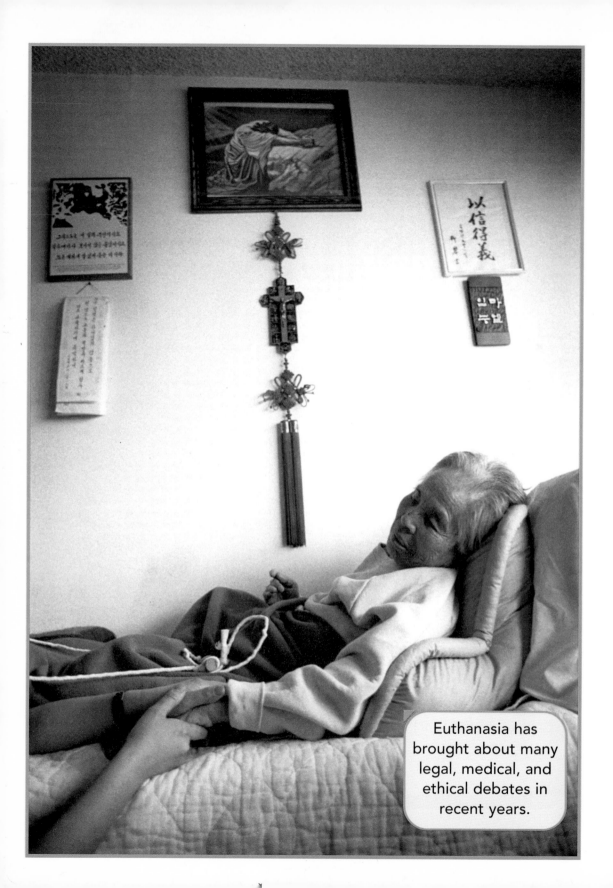

Euthanasia has brought about many legal, medical, and ethical debates in recent years.

EUTHANASIA

The Debate Over the Right to Die

Seamus Cavan

The Rosen Publishing Group, Inc.
New York

Published in 2000 by The Rosen Publishing Group, Inc.
29 East 21st Street, New York, NY 10010

Copyright © 2000 by The Rosen Publishing Group, Inc.

First Edition

Library of Congress Cataloging-in-Publication Data

Cavan, Seamus.
    Euthanasia / by Seamus Cavan.
      p. cm. — (Focus on science and society)
    Includes bibliographical references and index.
    ISBN 0-8239-3215-X (lib. bdg. : alk. paper) 1. Euthanasia—Juvenile
literature. [1.Euthanasia.] I. Title. II. Series.
R726 .C3876 2000
179.7—dc21   00-009392

Manufactured in the United States of America

CONTENTS

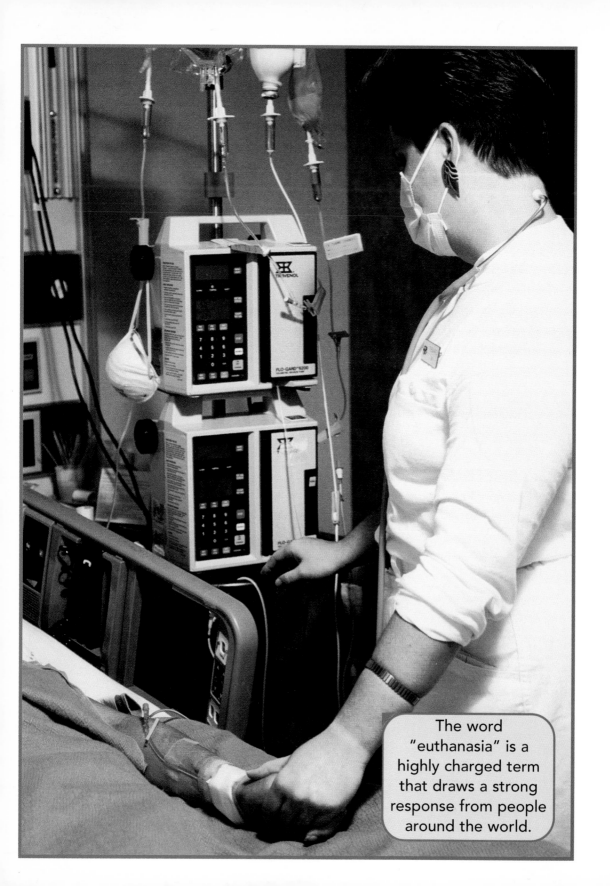

The word "euthanasia" is a highly charged term that draws a strong response from people around the world.

A SIMPLE WORD, A DIFFICULT QUESTION

Translated literally, the word means "a good death." According to P. C. Munson, a lawyer in the state of Oregon—a center of the legal battle over it in recent years—"it is becoming the abortion issue of the next century and [the controversy is] just as nasty....Yet it is even more important because how we die concerns absolutely everyone." Gary Abrams, a medical ethicist and journalist who has written extensively on the subject, says, "It is absolutely the moral, legal, philosophical, and ethical issue of the next millennium. Society is going to have to face it, in all its aspects, no matter how difficult, unpleasant, or distasteful that may prove to be. And that's not just in the United States but around the world."

Here in the United States, the flamboyant—some would say ghoulish—physician Dr. Jack Kevorkian, who made this issue his cause, became one of the most famous people in the country and the object of frequent prosecution—persecution, his defenders would say—by law enforcement agencies and the government. Geoffrey Feiger, the lawyer who defended Dr. Kevorkian in Michigan, the state where the doctor had focused his crusade, was able to use the fame he had gained from his association with Dr. Kevorkian to mount a successful campaign to gain the nomination of the state Democratic Party for governor. He even came close to winning the election!

So what is the "it" that we're talking about? It is euthanasia, a word derived from two ancient Greek words: *eu,* which means good or easy, and *thanatos,* which means death. Euthanasia, therefore, means literally "a good death" or "an easy death," in the sense of a death without pain or suffering.

But the word seems to mean a good deal more. It is a highly charged term that draws strong, heartfelt responses from just about everyone. To its advocates, it is an act of mercy, kindness, and compassion. To those who oppose it, it is an act of murder.

Indeed, the most common definition of euthanasia combines aspects of both these views. Asked for a definition of euthanasia, most people would say, simply, that euthanasia is mercy killing. But when asked whether euthanasia is good or bad, whether it should be legal or illegal, what society's position on it should be, and what role the medical profession should play in euthanasia, most people would provide much more complex answers.

Dr. Jack Kevorkian has made euthanasia his cause.

So what exactly is euthanasia? After all, to say that it is mercy killing does not really tell a person much. Why is it such a controversial issue, and why is it such a big deal today? Is it a new issue? Why is it likely to become even more fiercely debated in the near future? Why is it society's concern, as opposed to being simply the private business of individuals? Is euthanasia suicide? Is it murder? Is it, or should it be, a crime? Are there specific circumstances under which it is, or should be, a crime?

EUTHANASIA

As you may have gathered from what you have already read, or as you may have already known, different people have very different answers to all of these questions. The answers to these questions directly reflect some of the deepest mysteries and questions that human beings have wrestled with throughout history: What is life? What is death? Who, if anyone, has the right to make that determination, including oneself?

It is not the purpose of this book to provide you with answers to these questions. That would be both impossible and inappropriate. Instead, we hope to provide you with enough basic information about this extremely complex and sensitive issue to help you start thinking intelligently about it on your own. In this sense, this book is just an introduction to the subject.

Timeline

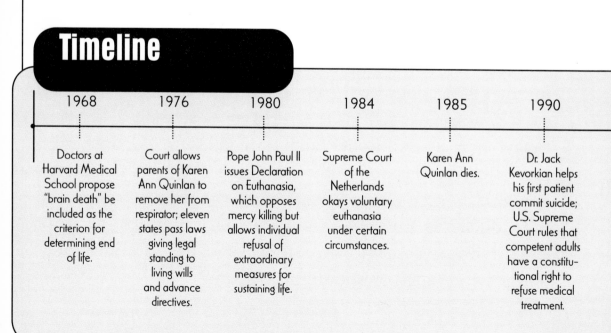

1968	1976	1980	1984	1985	1990
Doctors at Harvard Medical School propose "brain death" be included as the criterion for determining end of life.	Court allows parents of Karen Ann Quinlan to remove her from respirator; eleven states pass laws giving legal standing to living wills and advance directives.	Pope John Paul II issues Declaration on Euthanasia, which opposes mercy killing but allows individual refusal of extraordinary measures for sustaining life.	Supreme Court of the Netherlands okays voluntary euthanasia under certain circumstances.	Karen Ann Quinlan dies.	Dr. Jack Kevorkian helps his first patient commit suicide; U.S. Supreme Court rules that competent adults have a constitutional right to refuse medical treatment.

A SIMPLE WORD, A DIFFICULT QUESTION

Admittedly, euthanasia is a difficult and, in some ways, a depressing subject. Few people like to spend a lot of time thinking about death. But as a concerned and thoughtful young citizen, you will, in the future, most likely have reason to form an opinion on some, if not all, of these questions. We hope that this book provides a good starting point for your thinking.

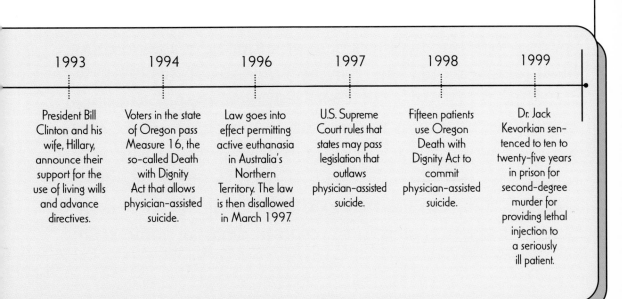

1993	1994	1996	1997	1998	1999
President Bill Clinton and his wife, Hillary, announce their support for the use of living wills and advance directives.	Voters in the state of Oregon pass Measure 16, the so-called Death with Dignity Act that allows physician-assisted suicide.	Law goes into effect permitting active euthanasia in Australia's Northern Territory. The law is then disallowed in March 1997.	U.S. Supreme Court rules that states may pass legislation that outlaws physician-assisted suicide.	Fifteen patients use Oregon Death with Dignity Act to commit physician-assisted suicide.	Dr. Jack Kevorkian sentenced to ten to twenty-five years in prison for second-degree murder for providing lethal injection to a seriously ill patient.

CHAPTER 2

WHAT IS EUTHANASIA?

The dictionary gives a simple definition for euthanasia: "the act or practice of killing or permitting the death of hopelessly sick or injured individuals (such as persons or domestic animals) in a relatively painless way for reasons of mercy."

Seems relatively simple to understand, doesn't it? And when you first think about it, it might even seem as if euthanasia should not be that controversial an act. After all, sparing someone needless pain or suffering is a good thing, most people would say. (For the purposes of this book, we are going to discuss euthanasia only as it applies to human beings, not animals.) If a person is hopelessly ill or hurt, with no hope of ever getting better; if he or she is in unbearable and unending pain, unable to enjoy or experience the things in life that give it meaning; if the person's illness or injury is certain to result in death at some point;

is it not an act of mercy—even of kindness—to let, or help, that person die?

This question is the essence of the euthanasia debate. Advocates of euthanasia would say simply that the answer is yes. (An advocate is someone who argues in favor of a certain position or point of view.) Advocates of euthanasia would argue that, provided that certain conditions are met (we will discuss those conditions later), euthanasia is an acceptable act that should not be considered illegal, immoral, or unethical. Because euthanasia is so often discussed in the context of the law and religion, they would say that, under the right circumstances, euthanasia should not be regarded as a sin, a moral offense, or a crime.

Opponents of euthanasia offer many arguments against this point of view. In general, these arguments center around the notion that no matter what criteria or definitions are offered for the circumstances under which euthanasia would become acceptable, real life is always much more difficult to categorize. As a result, any legal or moral standards that allow societies or individuals to move away from the protection of life offer potential for abuse, misunderstandings, and mistakes. From such a point of view, traditional legal, social, moral, and religious concepts that emphasize the sacredness of life and offer safeguards for it, even under the most drastic and sometimes painful circumstances, remain justified and necessary. In fact, such safeguards, the argument goes, are the very foundation of a legal and civilized society. To allow exceptions to them, as any concept of euthanasia does, is to chip away at the foundation of society itself.

Euthanasia's Legal Status Today

It should be noted that in most societies today, including Canada and most of the United States, the prevailing legal position is the traditional one, which opposes legal euthanasia. This is the case in virtually every country around the world, with the exception of the Netherlands, where euthanasia is legal under certain very specific conditions. Almost everywhere else, it is a crime.

In Germany, Switzerland, Norway, Uruguay, and some states in the United States, euthanasia is not legal, but it is not specifically a crime under the legal and penal code of those places. What this means is that a person charged with homicide in those nations could offer what essentially amounts to a "euthanasia defense." Most such cases involve someone who is terminally ill (meaning that he or she has a disease that is certain to result in death) or who is in extraordinary pain or suffering and is either killed or allowed to die by a friend, family member, or physician. In most such cases, the sick person has asked for this other person's help in ending his or her life in order to be "put out of his or her misery" and relieved of pain or suffering. In those places

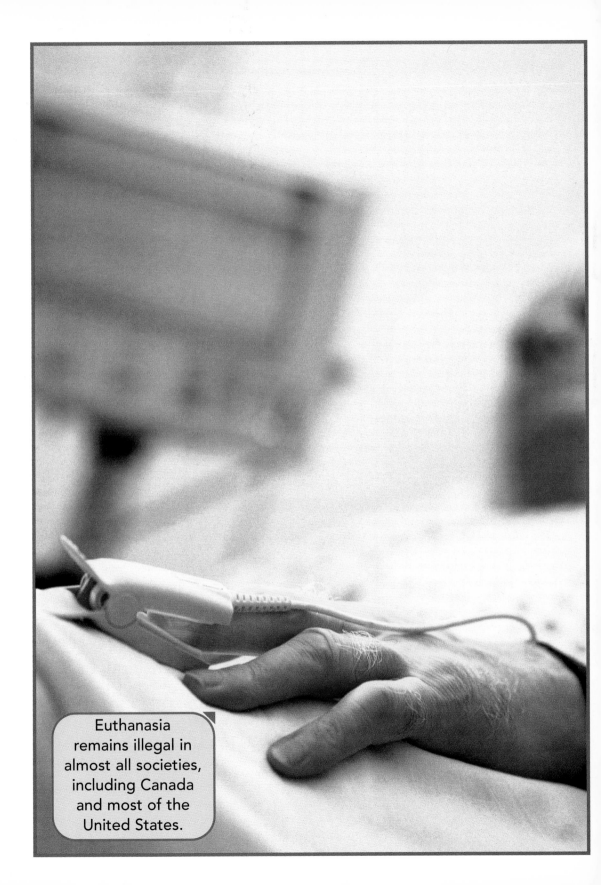

Euthanasia remains illegal in almost all societies, including Canada and most of the United States.

where euthanasia is not technically illegal, a person charged with a crime under such circumstances could cite these circumstances in his or her defense.

Each state must pass laws that either ban or decriminalize euthanasia.

But in the United States today, for example, euthanasia cannot, strictly speaking, be used as a defense against homicide. According to a Supreme Court decision, physician-assisted suicide is not a right guaranteed by the Constitution. That means it is up to each state to pass laws that either ban physician-assisted suicide or decriminalize it. So far, Oregon is the only state to pass a law to decriminalize physician-assisted suicide. Even in Oregon, there are very strictly defined circumstances under which euthanasia is not a crime. Although there have been several highly publicized cases—most notably those involving Dr. Kevorkian—in which euthanasia has been offered as a defense against a legal charge of homicide, such cases depend on a legal theory called "jury nullification." A lawyer and client who are depending on jury nullification are hoping that the jury is so sympathetic or understanding of their position or circumstances that it acts against the letter of the law by setting it aside. Jury nullification certainly occurs, but it does not change the fact that, under the law in most places in the United States, euthanasia is still a crime—an act of murder, in fact.

Public Opinion

It is interesting to note that although the legal status of euthanasia has not changed much in the United States and elsewhere, public opinion polls in recent years show a consistently strong—and growing—measure of support, at least in theory, for euthanasia. At the end of the 1990s, national polls conducted jointly by the television news network CNN and the newspaper *USA Today* show rates of public support in the United States for euthanasia "under certain circumstances" as ranging anywhere from 57 to 75 percent.

Although the degree of support varies greatly depending on how the question is phrased, recent polls in other nations show a similar, even sometimes greater measure of support—again, at least in theory and under certain circumstances. In Canada, for example, a nationwide Gallup Poll in 1995 showed support for euthanasia at 76 percent.

This was a dramatic rise from the 45 percent support recorded in 1968. Polls in Great Britain have shown support as high as 80 percent. In Australia, where euthanasia was briefly legal in one territory in the late 1990s, 81 percent of the population favored it under certain circumstances. In the Netherlands, home to the world's only national euthanasia statute, 92 percent of those polled believed that euthanasia should be a legal option under certain circumstances.

The situation in France regarding euthanasia is typical in many ways of the debate in most of the industrialized nations. In France today, euthanasia remains illegal, although indications of public support for euthanasia, under certain specific circumstances, leave lawmakers, ethicists, and members of the public conceding that the legal situation could change in the near future.

In March 2000, the National Ethics Committee of France issued its long-awaited report on euthanasia. The committee is charged with studying and reporting on ethical issues that affect medicine, science, law, and society, and its recommendations often serve as guidelines for lawmakers. In its report on euthanasia, the committee recommended that for the time being, euthanasia should still be treated as a crime under the legal system. But it admitted that under certain circumstances, the law may have to change. According to Dr. Didier Sicard, the head of the committee, if a person is terminally ill and "if palliative

DR. DEATH

Undoubtedly, the most controversial figure in the debate over euthanasia is Dr. Jack Kevorkian, who has helped more than 100 seriously ill people commit suicide. To them as well as many others, Kevorkian is a compassionate and courageous physician, even a savior. But to his opponents, Kevorkian is something much worse: an opportunist who takes advantage of sorrow and tragedy, and maybe even a murderer.

In the late 1980s, using $30 worth of spare parts, Kevorkian built a "suicide machine" that allowed a person, by pressing a button, to dispense a lethal dose of medication to himself or herself.

Between 1990 and 1998, Kevorkian helped more than 100 people commit suicide. Although all of his patients were seriously ill, not all were considered to be terminally ill.

During that time, Kevorkian was unsuccessfully prosecuted several times for murder in his home state of Michigan. He also had his medical license revoked, and the state passed legislation that outlawed physician-assisted suicide. Kevorkian persisted with his work until November 1998, when the television program *60 Minutes* broadcast a videotape of him giving a lethal injection to a fifty-two-year-old man who wished to die. Three days later, Kevorkian was arrested and charged with murder. This time he was convicted and sentenced to ten to twenty-five years in prison.

care and painkillers are ineffective, if all treatment or therapy has failed, if there is unanimous agreement that the situation has become intolerable, then one can envisage euthanasia."

The recommendation of the French committee seems to reflect the situation in much of the world, including the United States. That is, to judge by the laws in effect, society seems to believe that euthanasia should be illegal, but at the same time concedes the possibility that under some circumstances it may be permissible.

Whose Choice Is It?

So if the numbers in such polls are accurate, why is the practice of euthanasia not more widespread, and why isn't it legal in more places?

To begin with, it is important to remember that the results of such polls depend greatly upon the way the questions are phrased. A slight change in the wording of the poll can change the results immensely. It is also safe to say that with an issue as controversial as euthanasia, those who respond to the poll are responding to a theoretical proposition. Faced with all the complexities of the issue in real life, their response might be quite different. Certainly it has proved much more difficult to draft laws that voters agree with that allow euthanasia than it has been to get a majority of a population to speak in favor of euthanasia for the purposes of an opinion poll.

As for the practice of euthanasia, its legal status is certainly not a reflection of how, how often, and under which circumstances it takes place in the real world. As we all know, making something illegal does not guarantee that it will never occur. If this were the case, there would be no need for prisons, police, or criminal courts of law. No matter how you feel about euthanasia, it is undeniable that acts of euthanasia take place all the time.

There is no way to know how often this occurs, of course. The fact that euthanasia remains illegal and, to a certain extent, taboo (meaning "morally forbidden") helps ensure that when it is practiced, it remains a secret. However, many people who are in enormous pain or who are terminally ill make the decision to end their own lives in order to avoid further suffering and indignity. Sometimes they ask for help in carrying out this decision, either from someone they trust or from a physician. Whether they have the right to make such a decision is at the heart of the present-day euthanasia debate.

CHAPTER 3

MURDER VERSUS SUICIDE

It is safe to say that virtually every society has beliefs and rules that make it wrong for one individual to kill another. Although most societies provide for circumstances under which killing may be justified—self-defense, protecting someone, for honor or revenge, as legal punishment, as an act of war, as the accidental outcome of enforcing the law —most societies regard killing as both legally and morally wrong. All of these societies also provide for ways that killers should be punished.

In addition, aside from their legal or social codes, most societies also have a moral code that makes killing taboo. In many cases, even in secular societies such as the United States and Canada, that moral code draws upon religious and spiritual foundations. In general, such religious and spiritual beliefs regard life as a gift from God or some

KAREN ANN QUINLAN

Perhaps more than any other single incident, it was the tragic case of Karen Ann Quinlan that sparked the contemporary debate over euthanasia in the United States.

In April 1975, Quinlan, a native of New Jersey, was a twenty-one-year-old college student. After going to a party at which she apparently drank alcohol and took some tranquilizers, Quinlan collapsed and stopped breathing at least twice, both times for fifteen minutes or more. Doctors were able to revive her both times, but she suffered irreversible brain damage.

Legally and medically, Quinlan was still alive, since there was still brain activity, but she was in what doctors characterized as "a chronic persistent vegetative state," which means that her brain had no "cognitive function." In other words, Quinlan was without any consciousness or awareness of herself, her surroundings, or her situation. She was alive only in the sense that she was breathing, which doctors said she was capable of doing only with the help of a respirator. According to the doctors, there was absolutely no hope of recovery or improvement, and Karen would have to spend the rest of her life hooked to life-support machinery in the intensive care unit of a hospital.

Karen's parents asked her doctors to remove her from the respirator. They believed that their daughter would not have wanted to "live" in such a condition. The doctors refused, saying that removal would be equivalent to killing Karen. The Quinlans went to court, and the New Jersey Supreme Court agreed with them. Karen was removed from the respirator, but not from the feeding tubes. To the surprise of her physicians, Karen proved able to breathe on her own. She survived in her "persistent vegetative state" in a nursing home until June 1985, when she died of complications from pneumonia.

divine creator or power and hold that only this creator has the right to take away life. According to such thinking, to kill or take a life is an affront against God or nature, an immoral act, or a sin.

Like one's beliefs on any number of topics, such religious, moral, and spiritual beliefs may concur in virtually every way with the law or legal system that governs the society, or they may diverge in any number of key ways. You can probably think of some examples.

Consider this one: The legal system of virtually every modern state recognizes a specific circumstance under which it not only regards killing as legal but compels its citizens to kill on its behalf. Can you think of such a circumstance? During times of war, many countries rely on laws that allow them to draft (force) citizens, usually young men, into the armed forces and make them fight. Such fighting inevitably means killing.

In most societies, to refuse to serve in the nation's military when drafted is a crime. Even so, there are always individuals who refuse to serve, either because of personal moral and spiritual reasons or because of their belief in the teachings of a specific religious group. They may simply believe that killing and war are wrong under all circumstances or that the government is wrong in pursuing a particular war. They may belong to a religious group such as the Society of Friends, or Quakers, that teaches that one should not take up arms on behalf of the government.

Individuals who take such stances are sometimes prosecuted as criminals, and they can be treated by the rest of society as outcasts. Yet when times change, they may be seen as heroes. Such is the case with a group of young German students during World War II, known as the White Rose resistance. They courageously and publicly

The White Rose resistance opposed the Nazi government.

announced their opposition to Germany's murderous Nazi government, which was then engaged in an attempt to exterminate all of Europe's 11 million Jews. In their opposition to the Nazis, the members of the

White Rose were certainly in the minority in Germany, and they were arrested, tried, and executed as criminals. Today, however, they are regarded as heroes of conscience.

Whose Life Is It?

The point is that what a society allows or condemns under its legal code may or may not coincide with the individual moral and spiritual beliefs of its members. And although killing is probably as close to a universal moral taboo as there is, there are certainly circumstances in every society under which killing is not only allowed but is encouraged. Virtually every society, for example, pays great honor to its warriors or soldiers.

War is one widespread, well-known exception to the taboo against killing. One significant point about this exception is that it reflects a society's decision that under these specific circumstances, killing will be allowed. Other laws that allow killing under specific circumstances—protecting oneself against a crime, or a police officer apprehending a violent criminal—also represent society's determination that there are circumstances under which killing can be allowed.

Society, through its laws and its government, determines the circumstances under which an individual may kill. It is difficult to think of a general circumstance under which society leaves it up to an individual person to determine when killing might be justified. In general, society reserves for itself the right to kill—for example, as punishment for a criminal act—and grants dispensations to individuals to violate this taboo under specific circumstances. Those who violate society's rules about killing are subject to punishment as criminals.

There is one circumstance in today's world, however, under which an individual may kill without fear of legal retribution. That circumstance is suicide, or the killing of oneself. Although in the United States there is still a powerful moral, religious, and social taboo regarding suicide, there is little that the law or government can do to prevent a person from killing him- or herself or to legally punish a person who attempts to commit suicide.

For instance, most of the dominant religious and spiritual traditions from which American culture draws—including Christianity, Judaism, and Islam—still regard suicide as a sinful act. In such traditions, life is a gift bestowed by the creator, and only the creator may rightfully take it; whatever course one's life takes, one is bound morally to live it out until its end. Catholicism, for example, regards suicide as a mortal sin no less serious than murder. In many places, a Catholic who commits suicide may not be allowed a burial in the consecrated ground of a Catholic cemetery. The folk traditions of many of the cultures that make up the North American mosaic call for a person who commits suicide to be buried at a crossroads—a shared tradition reflected in cul-

tural sources as diverse as the blues music of rural African Americans in the South in the late nineteenth and early twentieth centuries and the Scandinavian and Central European immigrant settlers of the Great Plains.

The point of the crossroads as the burial site is that a crossroads is, by definition, a busy place or intersection, a place where much human interaction takes place. The soul of a person buried there will therefore be unable to rest, which is its punishment for seeking to escape from life before its allotted time.

Likewise, in some Native American cultures, people who have committed suicide are buried facing east, away from the setting sun and the "western lands" believed to be the domain of the spirit world and the site of the afterlife. That way the spirit is condemned to remain among the living.

The belief that suicide is wrong is still a very powerful one in this society. However, in the United States and most countries, the law no longer reflects this belief. Until well into the twentieth century in most places, suicide was illegal. How could someone who committed suicide be legally punished, you may be wondering? In most places, the answer is that the law prevents the person's heirs from inheriting whatever money or property he or she has left behind. This could be a very strong incentive against committing suicide.

Today, however, suicide is no longer illegal in most places, and society generally recognizes that whether people regard it as shameful, wrong, tragic, or immoral, suicide is essentially a private act, one that the law is relatively powerless to prevent.

So what does this discussion about legal and social attitudes about murder and suicide have to do with science and society's debate about euthanasia? Social attitudes toward euthanasia tend to be more positive the more the act is seen purely as an individual decision—an act of suicide—and less as an act that is subject to outside coercion or interference. In the latter case, euthanasia is seen as more closely resembling an act of murder. But in order to examine this proposition, we first have to look at a little bit of history and establish some definitions.

CHAPTER 4

"LIFE UNWORTHY OF LIFE"

At different times throughout history, some societies have regarded suicide as an acceptable, even honorable, act under certain circumstances. The ancient Greeks and Romans, for example, regarded suicide as an allowable or rightful alternative to massive dishonor or disgrace, as did traditional Japanese society.

One of the societies that practiced euthanasia on a large scale was Nazi Germany, when Germany was under the rule of Adolf Hitler shortly before and during its involvement in World War II (1939–1945). In many ways, the Nazi practice of euthanasia has helped to shape and determine the terms of today's debate.

Applied Biology

Nazi ideology, or belief, rested on a foundation of racial superiority. To create his murderous philosophy, Hitler drew on long-standing European and German traditions of anti-Semitism; corrupted understandings and applications of various scientific theories, especially evolution; and certain strains of German philosophy, historical theory, mythology, and folk tradition that he adapted for his own purposes.

Hitler and the other Nazis applied their own understandings of Darwin's theory of evolution and "the survival of the fittest" concept to history in the context of the struggle for power among nations and peoples. The survival of the fittest concept describes the evolutionary struggle for survival of animal and plant species in nature and the wild. Hitler proposed warfare as the determinant of the fitness of members of the human species, which he divided into races.

According to the Nazi view, the fittest of all the races was the Germans, or Aryans, as Hitler called them. He saw all of European history as reaching a climax during his reign, which he believed to be the beginning of the Third German Reich, or empire. Hitler thought that this Reich was destined to last one thousand years. Germany's fitness to survive would be proven and determined by its success on the battlefield, particularly in the titanic war against the Slavic peoples of Eastern Europe, especially Poland and Russia. German victory over these peoples was to provide the fitter or superior race, the Aryans, with the *Lebensraum*, or living space, that it supposedly needed in order to prosper, expand, and fulfill its historical destiny.

Nazi ideology rested on a notion of Aryan superiority and sought to eliminate people that the Nazis deemed less worthy of living.

EUTHANASIA

In Hitler's thinking, a nation or society could be seen both as an individual organism and as a species. "Nazism is simply applied biology," explained one high official of the regime. Accordingly, the ultimate Aryan triumph could be ensured only by the elimination of all those elements that would weaken the German people or make them less "fit." Foremost among these elements, according to Hitler, were the Jews, whom he made the scapegoats for everything that was wrong with German society.

Although at the start of Hitler's reign in 1933, Jews constituted just 1 percent of the German population, this did not make them any less dangerous to the German people, Hitler argued. "The great triumph of Nazism is the discovery of the Jewish virus," Hitler once proclaimed. According to Hitler's theory, just as a virus is no less dangerous because it cannot be seen by the naked eye, Jews were no less dangerous to the German people because of their small numbers. Further, just as an untreated virus can undermine the health of the organism in which it lives, so too would the Jews, without special treatment, undermine the health, strength, and fitness of the German people and empire. As the world now knows, the "special treatment" that Hitler attempted to apply to the "Jewish virus" was the extermination—mass murder—of all the Jews of Europe.

Preparation for the Unthinkable

Before Hitler and the Nazis put their Final Solution of the Jewish problem into effect, they took steps to desensitize the German people to the prospect of murder on such an unthinkable scale. One method of preparation was the relentless use of propaganda. Another important method of desensitization was a widespread program of euthanasia, which was intended to get the German people accustomed to the notion that some lives are not as worthy as others.

Although it was the elite secret police and intelligence arm of the Nazi party, known as the SS (an abbreviation of the German name for the Nazi organization *Schutzstaffel*, which literally means "protection squad"), that was primarily responsible for carrying out the Final Solution, the medical profession was Hitler's accomplice in the euthanasia program.

The euthanasia program initially grew out of Hitler's scheme to purify and strengthen the German people by forcibly sterilizing the "feeble-minded and the weak"—primarily the mentally retarded and the mentally ill—to ensure that they would never have children, pass on their "defects," and weaken the Aryan race.

But at the start of World War II, in September 1939, six large German hospitals, or sanatoriums, were converted into killing centers. The justification was that such individuals had to be killed not only to be saved from a life of suffering, pain, and misery, but also for the greater good of the German people. Such individuals, in the Nazi way of thinking, constituted "life unworthy of life." They were not the "fittest," so they did not deserve to survive, particularly in a time of war when resources were scarce and individual sacrifices had to be made for the

Over 100,000 people were killed in the Nazi's euthanasia program.

greater good of all German people. Because these groups' disabilities made them unfit for the armed forces, the Nazis argued, euthanasia served the function for these people that warfare served for the rest of society—to ensure the survival of the fittest members of the society.

Targeted for euthanasia were the mentally ill, particularly those suffering from schizophrenia or chronic depression; the mentally retarded; and the physically disabled (unless the disability resulted from injury suffered in German military service during World War I). Doctors were responsible for selecting those patients who were to be euthanized, carrying out the injections at the killing centers, and generating the paperwork that provided a medically credible cause of death for the surviving family members.

Both children and adults were selected for euthanasia. The SS established front organizations known as the General Ambulance Service, Charitable Sick Transports, and the Charitable Foundation for Institutional Care. These organizations transported patients to the six killing centers, "cared for" them while there, and funded and administered the program. Initially, euthanasia was accomplished by lethal injection or, particularly in the case of children, slow starvation. Later, with the need for greater numbers and efficiency of killing, the use of poison gas was pioneered. Ultimately, poison gas would become the preferred method of killing Jews in the death camps. More than 100,000 human beings were exterminated in the Nazi euthanasia program.

CHAPTER 5

WHO DECIDES?

Obviously, euthanasia advocates today do not support any program that remotely resembles the Nazi scheme. By any responsible moral standard presented in today's debates, what the Nazis were practicing was clearly murder in that individuals, representing the government or state, were deciding and acting to end another person's life with no pretense of consideration of that individual's wishes or his or her right to life. What today's euthanasia advocates support is the right of an individual to end his or her life—to commit suicide, in effect—when injury or illness makes that life, in that individual's opinion, no longer worth living.

Euthanasia advocates emphasize that the only person who can or should make the decision is the individual himself or herself. They propose various ways to ensure that this is always the case and to protect the individual making that decision from interference or coercion from any and all outside forces.

Although some euthanasia advocates speak of a "right to die" or a "right to death with dignity," most would agree that euthanasia should be limited to certain specific circumstances. Many would agree that under most circumstances, suicide is an unwise or perhaps even wrongful or immoral act. They would be quick to add, however, that it is a decision that can be made only by the individual in question and that society, in the form of government or the law, generally has no business getting involved.

Likewise, many opponents of euthanasia would sympathize with the desire of an individual in a painful and medically hopeless situation to exercise control over his or her own situation and life. Some might even agree that an individual in that tragic situation has the right to make a private, personal decision about his or her destiny.

Even some of those who regard suicide as wrong or immoral are not always so quick to condemn an individual who determines to cut short what he or she sees as a hopeless and pain-filled situation. Anybody who has watched a loved one endure a terminal illness, a catastrophic injury, or a medical condition with no hope of recovery knows that it is difficult to apply any absolute judgments to such a situation unless you are directly involved in it yourself. One can hold such a viewpoint, however, without necessarily believing that euthanasia should be a legal option.

Obviously, there is little room for agreement between advocates of euthanasia and those who hold that suicide is wrong under any circumstances. There would seem, however, to be some common ground between euthanasia advocates and those who would concede that, in some circumstances, suicide should be regarded as essentially a private decision.

Progress

Why then does euthanasia remain such a divisive issue, with neither side willing to yield any ground? In part, much of the bitterness of the debate arises from the immense progress in science and medicine that has been made in this century. In the most economically fortunate societies of the world, people are living longer than ever before. Although there are still a large number of fatal diseases that cannot be cured, there have been tremendous breakthroughs in treating such illnesses. These breakthroughs allow even people who are seriously ill to live much longer than they would have in the past.

What such progress means is a change not only in how long people live but also in the way that they die. When compared with people of the past, Americans today are

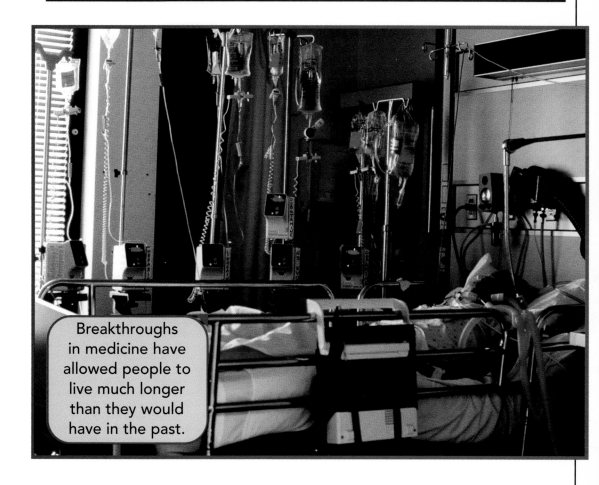

Breakthroughs in medicine have allowed people to live much longer than they would have in the past.

much more likely to die in a hospital while receiving the benefit of advanced medical care, their life extended by all kinds of new medical treatments. The same is true of citizens of other countries that are also wealthy enough to provide sophisticated medical care to a large percentage of their population.

Such progress also means, increasingly, that euthanasia is less likely to be a purely private and personal decision. Quite naturally, even the most seriously ill people want to take advantage of the wonders of medicine and science to live a meaningful life for as long as possible. For most people, it is only when all hope is gone, when pain and helplessness have removed all meaning from life, that they consider euthanasia. By this point, however, the vast majority of people are under a physician's care, usually in a hospital. Often they have become disabled to the point where they are unable to take steps on their own to end their life.

At this point, euthanasia advocates maintain, people should be able to call upon medical assistance to help them end their own lives. For those who oppose euthanasia, this is the point at which they consider euthanasia, no matter how it is defined or practiced, to be more akin to murder than to suicide. And it is on this point that the argument rests today, seemingly without resolution.

Some Terms

At this point, you need to know some terminology that is commonly used in today's debate over euthanasia. Advocates of euthanasia draw a number of important distinctions between the ways that it might be practiced.

Involuntary euthanasia describes the killing of a person in opposition to his or her wishes. A prime example would be euthanasia as practiced by the Nazis.

Passive euthanasia refers to hastening the death of a sick person by withdrawing some form of treatment from him or her and letting nature take its course. Examples include removing life-support equipment, such as turning off a respirator; stopping other medical procedures; halting food and water to a patient in a coma; and not resuscitating a patient whose heart has stopped.

Active euthanasia

involves taking a positive step or direct action to bring about the death of another person. It differs from involuntary euthanasia in that this

Physician-assisted suicide is done at the request of a terminally ill person.

step is taken at the request of the sick person. An example would be Dr. Kevorkian's killing, by lethal injection at the request of the patient, of an individual suffering from ALS, also known as Lou Gehrig's disease, in 1998.

EUTHANASIA

Physician-assisted suicide describes the circumstance in which a doctor supplies the necessary information and the means of committing suicide to a patient who requests it. Commonly, this might be a lethal dose of sleeping pills or a method of administering carbon monoxide gas. Physician-assisted suicide is also sometimes referred to as voluntary passive euthanasia. The best-known example of physician-assisted suicide is, once again, that practiced by Dr. Kevorkian in the 1990s. Kevorkian devised two types of euthanasia or suicide machines. One hooks his patients to a machine that delivers a measured, lethal dose of medications when the patient presses a button. His second machine provides carbon monoxide and a face mask that allows the patient to initiate the flow of the poisonous gas.

THE IMPASSE

Physician-assisted suicide is the subject of the relatively small amount of existing legislation that permits euthanasia, such as the laws in Oregon and the Netherlands. Most of today's debate regarding euthanasia thus centers on physician-assisted or voluntary passive euthanasia. Advocates of physician-assisted suicide argue that it is possible to establish safeguards that would ensure that no one is forced into euthanasia against his or her will. What are such safeguards?

In general, advocates of euthanasia argue that an individual should be able to decide to end his or her life if the person:

- Is suffering from a terminal illness
- Is unlikely to benefit from the discovery of

a cure for that illness during the remainder of his or her life

■ Either suffers unbearable pain as a direct result of the illness, or is reduced to a way of life that has become unbearably burdensome in the sense that it leaves him or her overly dependent on others or on life-support technology

■ Has expressed a consistent, voluntary, and rational wish to die

■ Is unable to commit suicide without assistance

The Death with Dignity Act

As mentioned, Oregon is the only state that currently allows terminally ill patients the option of physician-assisted suicide. The Death with Dignity Act, as the Oregon law is called, was first approved by Oregon's voters in 1994, but legal challenges prevented it from taking effect until 1997.

The Oregon law allows a terminally ill patient to request a prescription for a lethal dose of fatal medications if the patient is:

■ At least eighteen years old

■ A resident of Oregon

- Capable of making rational decisions about his or her health care
- Diagnosed with a terminal illness that will lead to death within six months

Patients who meet these criteria can request a prescription for lethal medication from a licensed physician. To actually receive the prescription, the following conditions must be met:

- Patients must make two separate requests to their physician, separated by at least fifteen days.
- The patient must make the request in writing.
- The prescribing physician and a second consulting physician must confirm the patient's diagnosis and prognosis. The consulting physician must determine that the patient is capable of making a rational decision about his or her future, in the sense that his or her judgment is unimpaired by any psychological or psychiatric condition.
- The prescribing physician must inform the patient of all reasonable alternatives to assisted suicide.

- The prescribing physician is required to ask the patient to notify his or her next of kin about the request for a lethal prescription. The patient, however, is not required to actually follow this order and notify his or her next of kin.

Under the Oregon law, doctors must report any prescriptions they write under the Death with Dignity Act to the Oregon Health Department. Moreover, physicians and health care systems are not required to participate in the Death with Dignity Act. As of 1999, twenty-three persons had received prescriptions for lethal medications under the act. Fifteen of those used the medications to end their own lives; thirteen of these people were suffering from cancer.

Euthanasia in the Netherlands

The legal status of euthanasia in the Netherlands has undergone an evolution in response to widespread public support (92 percent in one poll) for physician-assisted suicide. Until 1993, euthanasia was theoretically illegal. In that year a law was passed that protected doctors from prosecution for euthanasia under the following conditions:

- The patient is in unbearable pain, whether emotional, physical, or both.

THE IMPASSE

- The patient has made repeated rational requests to die.

- Two doctors agree that euthanasia is justified.

- The patient's family is consulted.

- The circumstances of the death are reported to the appropriate government and medical authorities.

Between 1993 and 1997, an estimated 3 percent of deaths that occurred in the Netherlands were the result of physician-assisted suicide. In 1997, new legislation was passed that completely decriminalized physician-assisted suicide. In certain circumstances, the Dutch law would allow individuals as young as twelve to request assistance in dying without the permission of their parents. Otherwise, the Dutch legislation permits physician-assisted suicide only if:

- The patient is suffering unbearably.

- The patient makes repeated voluntary, rational requests.

- There is no reasonable alternative.

- The doctor has advised the patient of his or her situation.

Many people hope that medical advances will eliminate pain and suffering—and therefore the need for euthanasia.

- At least one other independent physician has been consulted.
- All due medical care is to be followed.

Most proposed euthanasia legislation in other places follows similar guidelines.

The Argument Against

So what arguments are offered against physician-assisted suicide? The primary argument is, of course, that suicide under any circumstances is wrong. As mentioned earlier, this belief is widespread in many societies and is taught in many religions. However, even many religions with very strict teachings about suicide allow for exceptions in certain cases. For example, under specific conditions, the Catholic Church does not regard certain forms of so-called passive euthanasia to be suicide. The Church does not require terminally ill patients to resort to "extraordinary measures" to preserve life. An example of such extraordinary measures would be getting hooked up to life-support equipment.

A corollary is the belief that no life, no matter what the objective circumstances, is ever totally without hope. Again, this argument is frequently offered by those with strong religious convictions in the belief that life and death are mysteries that are only for God or a supreme being to resolve.

A related argument is that advances in health care, including the ready availability of new painkilling medications, mean that no patient ever has to suffer truly unbearable pain. This assumes, of course, that all patients have equal access to the same level of medical treatment, which given inequalities in income and access to health insurance is often not the case. In addition, advocates of euthanasia argue that the only person in the position to judge whether his or her pain is unbearable is the individual himself or herself.

It is also argued that physicians, whose job it is to heal, have no business being involved in bringing about death, even when it is in accordance with the patient's wishes. Similarly, it is argued that if physician-assisted suicide is made legal, doctors might feel compelled to provide such "treatment" for their patients, even if they are personally opposed to such action.

Advocates of euthanasia counter that relieving a patient's pain is part of the doctor's mission of healing and that when no other medical treatment remains, helping a patient to die thus becomes a medically ethical act. They also argue that, as with any medical procedure, physicians would never be compelled to provide a form of treatment in which they do not believe. Furthermore,

LIVING WILLS

The Karen Ann Quinlan case (see chapter 3) made many people think about what they would do—or would want to have done—if they were in a circumstance similar to that of Karen or her parents.

Medical technology has made it possible for people to survive virtually indefinitely with the help of life-support machinery. Many people, however, do not want to live under such conditions—that is, if they should become unable to live independent of life-support. Even many people whose religious faith determines their approach to this question believe that it is not sinful to not want to prolong one's life with such "extraordinary measures."

The law agrees, provided that it is the sick person whose wishes are being reflected. Obviously, it is impossible for many people in such drastic circumstances to communicate what they want. For example, Karen Ann Quinlan was unable to speak; in her particular case, a court of law was convinced that Karen's parents were acting as she would have wished.

Today, however, it is not necessary to go to court in such situations. All fifty states have laws that recognize the legal force of documents known as living wills or advance directives. Although the specific forms vary, a living will is a document that establishes, as specifically as possible, what sort of medical measures you would want taken if illness or injury left you unable to communicate your wishes. In some cases, the will simply designates a person to make such decisions for you. Such directives may also address which, if any, extraordinary measures a person would want used to sustain his or her life.

they maintain that the involvement of the medical profession is the best way to guarantee that euthanasia is always medically justified and never forced upon a patient.

Opponents counter by citing the example of Nazi Germany, where physicians helped Nazis carry out a program of involuntary euthanasia. They may be willing to concede that the likelihood of such abuses occurring in a democratic society, such as the United States or the Netherlands, is small, but they

Some people oppose physician-assisted suicide on religious grounds.

point out that the United States has performed medical experiments on people without their consent and even forcibly sterilized tens of thousands of mainly poor and disabled Americans in the early twentieth century.

THE IMPASSE

This leads to the final argument against even the most strictly regulated voluntary passive euthanasia, which draws from the reasoning already discussed and leaves opponents and advocates of euthanasia, once again, with little ground for agreement.

According to this argument, the very fact that a person is in the end stages of a terminal illness makes it unlikely, if not impossible, that his or her decision to die could meet any of the proposed criteria. They point out that being in the end stages of a terminal illness is by definition an extraordinary situation that makes it difficult or impossible to make a rational decision. People in such a position, they argue, are already faced with all kinds of pressure that make it more likely that they will choose death. They may be in extraordinary pain. They may feel humiliated or degraded by their inability to take care of themselves. They may feel as if they are a burden to their family or loved ones, in either an emotional or a financial sense. They may feel enormous financial pressure to end their life so as not to incur further medical costs. They are quite likely to be depressed, in the medical sense, by their situation and thereby unable to think clearly. Their judgment may be clouded by pain or medication.

No Solution?

Advocates of euthanasia often cite the testimony of terminally ill patients themselves, who explain that just having physician-assisted euthanasia available would be an enormous comfort to them. Many say that just knowing that such an option is available and legal would give them the strength to carry on all the way to the end without choosing euthanasia.

Opponents, however, argue that making any form of euthanasia legally available increases the likelihood that terminally ill patients will feel pressured to end their lives. As long as euthanasia is not available as a legal option, opponents state, the act remains unthinkable. Its legal unavailability therefore serves as a kind of refuge and protection for people who might otherwise feel compelled to choose euthanasia.

And there, for the present, the argument rests, certain to be revisited in courtrooms, the media, and hospitals many times in the near future. What do you think?

GLOSSARY

active euthanasia   Deliberate action to end the life of a dying patient to spare him or her further suffering.

active voluntary euthanasia   Lethal injection by a physician, at the request of an ill patient, to end the patient's life.

advocate   A person who argues in favor of a certain position or point of view.

living will   A written document, legal in all fifty states, in which a patient requests that a doctor disconnect him or her from life support (or not connect him or her at all) if the procedure will only delay eventual death.

passive euthanasia   The deliberate withdrawal of treatment (such as life-support equipment or procedures to resuscitate a person whose heart has stopped) from a sick patient in order to permit the person to die naturally.

EUTHANASIA

physician-assisted suicide (voluntary passive euthanasia)
Providing the drugs or other means by which a person can kill himself or herself.

suicide Deliberately ending one's own life.

taboo Something that is forbidden according to social morals and custom.

terminal illness An illness for which there is no known cure and that ultimately leads to death.

FOR MORE INFORMATION

In the United States

Pro-Euthanasia

Death with Dignity National Center
1818 N Street NW, Suite 450
Washington, DC 20036
(202)530-2900
e-mail: infor@deathwithdignity.org
Web site: http://www.deathwithdignity.org

Euthanasia Research and Guidance Organization (ERGO)
24829 Norris Lane
Junction City, OR 97448-9559
(541) 998-1873
e-mail: ergo@efn.org
Web site: http://www.rights.org/deathnet/ergo.html

Anti-Euthanasia

International Anti-Euthanasia Task Force
P.O. Box 760

Steubenville, OH 43952
(740) 282-3810
Web site: http://www.iaetf.org

National Right to Life Committee
419 7th Street NW, Suite 500
Washington, DC 20004
(202) 626-8800
e-mail: nrlc@nrlc.org
Web site: http://www.nrlc.org

In Canada

Pro-Euthanasia

Dying with Dignity
188 Eglinton Avenue East #705
Toronto, ON M4P 2X7
(416) 486-3998
e-mail: dwdca@web.apc.org
Web site: http://www.web.apc.org/dwd

Anti-Euthanasia

Euthanasia Prevention Coalition of BC
103-2609 Westview Drive, Suite 126
North Vancouver, BC V7N 4N2
(604) 794-3772
e-mail: info@epc.bc.ca
Web site: http://www.epc.bc.ca

FOR FURTHER
READING

Boyd, Sunni. *Euthanasia*. San Diego: Lucent Books, 1995.

De Koster, Katie. *Euthanasia*. San Diego: Greenhaven Press, 1999.

Frey, R.G., Gerald Dworkin, and Sissela Bok. *Euthanasia and Physician-Assisted Suicide*. New York: Cambridge University Press, 1998.

Leone, Daniel A. *The Ethics of Euthanasia*. San Diego: Greenhaven Press, 1998.

Manning, Michael. *Euthanasia and Physician-Assisted Suicide: Killing or Caring?* Mahwah, NJ: Paulist Press, 1998.

McCuen, Gary E. *Doctor Assisted Suicide and the Euthanasia Movement*. Hudson, WI: McCuen Publications, 1999.

Torr, James D. *Euthanasia: Opposing Viewpoints*. San Diego: Greenhaven Press, 2000.

INDEX

INDEX

CREDITS

About the Author

Seamus Cavan is a freelance writer. He is the author of many nonfiction books for young adult readers.

Photo Credits

Cover photo © Juan Silva/Image Bank; p. 2 © Dean Wong/ Corbis; p. 6 © Image Bank; p. 9 © AFP/ Corbis; p. 15 © Jeff Cadge/Image Bank; p. 16 © J. Pickerell/ FPG; p. 19 © Richard Sheinwald/AP Photo; p. 25 © George J. Wittenstein; p. 28 © Carol Havens/Corbis; pp. 33, 36 © United States Holocaust Museum; pp. 41, 43, 50 © Superstock; p. 54 © AP Photo.

Series Design

Mike Caroleo

Layout

Cynthia Williamson